Many Victorian cards featured designs with a historical influence, especially from the medieval period, as in this humorous unmarked card from the early 1880s. (105 mm x 80 mm)

CHRISTMAS CARDS

from the 1840s to the 1940s

Michelle Higgs

The Shire Book

Published in 1999 by Shire Publications Ltd,
Cromwell House, Church Street, Princes Risborough,
Buckinghamshire HP27 9AA, UK
(Website www.shirebooks.co.uk).

British Library Cataloguing in Publication Data:
Higgs, Michelle
Christmas cards. – (The Shire book)
1. Christmas cards – History 2. Christmas cards –
Collectors and collecting I. Title 741.6'84
ISBN 0 7478 0426 5

Cover: *(Top left) A Christmas card issued in the 1880s by Raphael Tuck & Sons. (Top right) An embossed folded card from the Edwardian period issued by Raphael Tuck & Sons. Inside, there is a short verse by Sir Walter Scott and a preprinted 'from'. (Bottom left) A Christmas postcard by C. W. Faulkner & Co, printed in Germany, postmarked 1910. (Bottom right) A small Christmas card issued by Goodall & Son in the 1860s.*

ACKNOWLEDGEMENTS
I would like to thank my husband, Carl, for taking the photographs for the illustrations
in this book, most of which are of cards from my collection. Exceptions are those on page 4
and page 5 (top), which are reproduced by permission of Birmingham Libraries, and those
on page 31, which are used by courtesy of Gareth Edwards.
Thanks are also due to my family, friends and colleagues who have given me invaluable
support and encouragement during the writing of this book, and to Sheila Coe for her
advice and assistance in adding to my collection.

Printed in Great Britain by CIT Printing Services Ltd,
Press Buildings, Merlins Bridge, Haverfordwest,
Pembrokeshire SA61 1XF.

CONTENTS

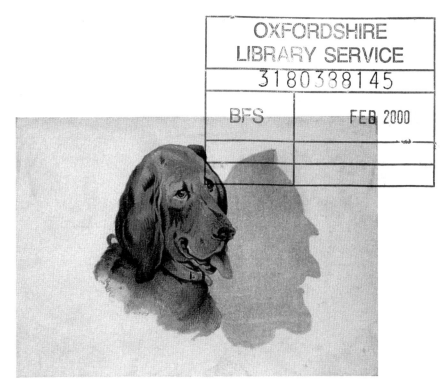

An unmarked 'shadow' card possibly from the early 1880s. This card shows a bloodhound casting a shadow very like that of Sherlock Holmes. Shadow cards drew parallels between human and animal characteristics. (105 mm x 74 mm)

Overview

When Charles Dickens wrote *A Christmas Carol* in 1843 the Christmas card had not been invented. This is surprising, since Dickens's story seems to encapsulate what we think of as the Victorian Christmas, but at the beginning of Queen Victoria's reign many customs now associated with the festive season, including the exchanging of cards, played no part in the celebrations.

However, the sending of seasonal messages of goodwill to friends and relatives is an ancient tradition, especially at New Year. It dates back to pagan times, when the exchange of good luck charms at the winter solstice was common. In the eighteenth century, New Year cards were sent on a commercial basis by tradesmen to their customers, but this was not a custom of the general public.

So what did the Victorians have in place of Christmas cards? The Christmas card as a decorative object and vehicle for sending seasonal messages has its origins in a number of different customs.

In the eighteenth century, children at school worked their 'Christmas Pieces' for their parents, which showed examples of their handwriting on paper with engraved borders. This practice continued well into the nineteenth century and, in about 1820, the pieces became more decorative and were enhanced with colour.

A development of this was the production of decorative notepaper. By the 1830s, quarto-sized pictorial headed notepaper was for sale in all major cities, seaside resorts and places of interest and was used especially at Christmas to write to friends and relatives. People making personal visits could dress up their visiting cards for the festive season with the addition of decorative scraps.

Another form of card that was adapted for Christmas by the addition of scraps was the colourful Reward card. These cards, which were

A card from the late 1850s that is similar to cards sent by tradesmen. 'Compliments' has been crossed out. (95 mm x 65 mm) (Reproduced by permission of Birmingham Libraries)

With Uncle John's
Love, ~~Compliments~~ 1859.
Wishing you a Merry X Mas
AND
A Happie New Year.

A Reward card from the late 1850s, one of the forerunners of the Christmas card. These highly decorative cards were given to Sunday school children to reward regular attendance. (94 mm x 60 mm) (Reproduced by permission of Birmingham Libraries)

A Valentine of the 1860s made up of paper 'lace' and scraps. Before the pre-printed Christmas card became popular, visiting cards were dressed up for the festive season using the same method. (92 mm x 119 mm)

printed with religious quotations, were given to children who attended Sunday school regularly.

An important forerunner of the Christmas card was the Valentine, which has a long pedigree and was immensely popular in the Victorian period. Valentines were a direct descendant of pictorial notepaper and were extremely decorative. Many early Christmas cards were issued by Valentine publishers using similar designs and motifs, such as cupids and flowers. Consequently, they do not seem very seasonal to the modern eye.

There are many contenders for the title of the world's first Christmas card but it is generally accepted that this was one sent in 1843 (probably soon after *A Christmas Carol* was written). It was commissioned by Sir Henry Cole, who later became the first director of the Victoria and Albert Museum. He asked John Calcott Horsley, a member of the Royal Academy, to design a card for him to send to his friends.

The card was lithographically printed by Jobbins of Warwick Court, Holborn, and each copy was hand-coloured by a professional colourer named William Mason. It was issued from the office of a periodical-cum-art shop called 'Felix Summerly's Home Treasury Office' by Joseph Cundall, a friend of Cole. Cundall believed that 'many copies were sold, but possibly not more than 1,000'. The cards were expensive items in those days, costing one shilling each, so Cole must have intended to make something of this business opportunity, rather than simply save time on writing Christmas messages to his friends.

Cole's card wished the recipient 'A Merry Christmas and a Happy New Year to You'. It featured a family of three generations partaking of good cheer (even the children!) and toasting the absent friend – the recipient. On either side were allegorical vignettes of charitable acts showing 'Clothing the Naked' and 'Feeding the Hungry'.

There are several other contenders for the title of the first Christmas card. William Maw Egley designed and produced a beautifully etched card that was similar to Horsley's design for Cole, with three arcaded panels portraying charitable acts. This was not issued until 1848, however, and is now widely acknowledged as the world's second Christmas card. Another contender is a card of W. C. T. Dobson, RA, who in 1844, a year after Cole's card, sent a sketch to a friend symbolising the spirit of Christmas. The following year, copies were lithographed and circulated but none was available commercially.

The invention of the envelope was an essential factor in ensuring the

The world's first Christmas card, commissioned by Sir Henry Cole and designed by his friend J. C. Horsley in 1843.

An early visiting-card type of Christmas card from the 1860s. It is ornately shaped, printed in black, gold and silver, and has a simple greeting in the centre. (94 mm x 60 mm)

Left and below: *Both sides of an envelope from the 1860s that is ornately printed in black. (95 mm x 65 mm)*

success of the Christmas card as the cards were designed to be sent in envelopes. It is believed that the first envelope was made in 1820 by a Mr Brewer, who owned a stationery shop in Brighton and catered for visitors from across the Channel. Warren De La Rue, the son of Thomas De La Rue, and Edwin Hill, brother of Rowland Hill, the originator of penny postage, patented the first envelope-making machine in the De La Rue works in 1844, and at a demonstration at the 1851 Great Exhibition the machine cut paper, folded and gummed 2700 envelopes in one hour using one operator. De La Rue

& Co later became an important Christmas card manufacturer. It has often been suggested that early Christmas cards were made specifically to fit these early envelopes.

Pictorial envelopes were issued to coincide with the launch of penny postage on 6th May 1840. William Mulready, RA, designed a pictorial envelope and lettersheet but they were withdrawn after strong press and public criticism. In December 1840 Fores of Piccadilly produced its

A popular style of card with the date 1876 on the reverse. The two panels open to reveal a third, typically Victorian picture of two children with a family of cats (illustrated below). (120 mm x 81 mm)

own version, which proved to be more successful.

However, it was the Christmas card that became the most popular of all – but not immediately. Although Cole's card was produced in 1843, the sending of pre-printed Christmas cards did not catch on until almost twenty years later. There are two main reasons for this: before the invention of the chromolithographic process, the production of cards was too expensive; and, in the years before the comprehensive reform of the postal service, delivery was costly.

An early form of colour printing was invented by George Baxter in the mid 1830s. The Baxter process involved the use of aquatinted foundation plates and oil colours printed from many separately engraved woodblocks, copper or zinc plates, or lithographic stones. Baxter patented his invention from 1835 to 1854 and, during the last five years of this period, he licensed the technique to a number of different printers. The licences were in use until the 1870s, and many early Christmas cards were produced by Baxter licensees.

The inside of the card illustrated above.

8

The Baxter process led naturally to the development of cheaper forms of colour reproduction, including chromolithography in about 1860, and other photographic processes. Lithography works on the principle that greasy oil and water have a mutual repulsion. The design is drawn in reverse with a greasy crayon or ink on to a block of limestone, zinc or aluminium and the block is soaked in water and inked. Paper is applied to the block, and the ink adheres to the paper not to the wet block.

In the early nineteenth century most people still delivered their messages and greetings by hand because delivery by post was expensive and few front doors even had letterboxes at this stage. Until the introduction of penny postage in May 1840, using an envelope had incurred double postage as postal rates were based on distance and the number of sheets of paper enclosed. Afterwards, for the first time, postage was paid in advance by the sender, not the recipient, and the rate was governed by weight – a penny for up to half an ounce (14 grams) and twopence for up to 2 ounces (57 grams).

In the 1850s and 1860s the number of Christmas cards sent by post was negligible, but after 1870 the custom became increasingly popular. The Post Office introduced a halfpenny stamp for postcards and, at the same time, decreed that Christmas cards (and letters) could also be sent for a halfpenny if they were enclosed in an unsealed envelope. During the 1870s the number of Christmas cards sent increased steadily every year, and by the 1880s it reached well into the millions.

In 1877 a correspondent to *The Times* complained about the 'social evil' of 'the delay of legitimate correspondence by cartloads of children's cards', and in that year it was estimated that four and a half million letters and cards were sent in the seven days before Christmas. In 1880 the Postmaster General thought it necessary to issue the first plea to 'Post Early for Christmas', but it was not until 1925 that last posting dates for Christmas were specified. Until 1960 there were postal deliveries on Christmas Day, although, owing to the increasing volume of mail, delivery was not guaranteed for Christmas unless the Postmaster's advice to post early was taken.

In the 1860s the most common type of Christmas card was a small chromolithograph similar to the size of a visiting card with a paper 'lace' border. In the 1870s folded cards without inserts started to appear but flat cards still dominated the Christmas card market. During the 1870s and 1880s cards increased in size and could be made in a variety of different shapes. Mechanical and 'tab' cards were particularly in vogue. Later, folded cards started to have inserts with a greeting and verse secured with a coloured cord or tassel that was tied around the card. From the 1890s

Below: *A card by Kate Greenaway, one of the most famous designers of Victorian Christmas cards. It was designed for Marcus Ward & Co and features two fairy children on a daffodil; it is one of a set of six produced in the late 1870s. (90 mm x 119 mm)*

Below left: Many Victorian Christmas cards were wonderfully humorous, as in this unmarked card, possibly from the 1870s, which pokes fun at the balancing act required to ride a penny farthing bicycle. (79 mm x 121 mm)

Below right: A larger Christmas card issued by Marcus Ward & Co. It has a popular animal scene and space for a name and dates from the 1880s, when cards were mass-produced for a less literate population. (111 mm x 150 mm)

coloured silk ribbons started to replace the cords, and from 1899 to 1900 the ribbon began to be secured through two holes on the left-hand side of the card and tied in a bow. However, the two types of card seem to have existed in tandem as there were many cards from the Edwardian period and the 1920s that were secured by a cord or ribbon around the card.

From the late 1870s and early 1880s designs for Christmas cards encompassed all manner of subjects from sentimental scenes of children and snowy landscapes through to comic capers and religious quotations. Christmas cards were sold in toy shops, tobacconists and drapery stores as well as bookshops and stationers.

Christmas stationery was first advertised in the *Illustrated London News* in 1863:

> A Merry Christmas and a Happy New Year! CHARLES GOODALL and SON'S remarkably beautiful series of designs in CHRISTMAS COMPLIMENTARY STATIONERY are to be had of GEORGE PHILIP and SON, 33 Fleet-street, E.C.

Cards were reviewed in the national press, as books are today, and newspapers printed lengthy advertisements detailing designs of cards in the run-up to Christmas. *The Times* in its issue of 18th December 1882 reviewed a number of cards produced by the main manufacturers, including Marcus Ward & Co:

> Birds and flowers are still happily illustrated in Messrs. Marcus Ward and Co.'s collection, but particular attention may be directed to a card in which portraits of a gallant and a dame of the days of Elizabeth are stepping from their frames to shake hands with each other in the presence of two youthful descendants.

Even so, at this stage Christmas cards were still luxuries only the

upper and middle classes could afford. They did not become affordable to the masses until early in the twentieth century when Christmas postcards became hugely popular; these did not require an envelope and were cheaper than the new folded cards.

At the same time, mass production brought the folded Christmas card within reach of a greater proportion of the population. New materials were used, such as parchment, celluloid and hand-coloured photographs. The cheaper cards had machine-stitched covers. Mass production coincided with a marked decline in the quality of cards, not merely in their design but also in their finish. However, there are many outstanding early twentieth-century Christmas card designs that reflect the tastes of the age.

In the Edwardian period card designs were strongly influenced by the Art Nouveau style. During the First World War the sending of cards took on a poignant new meaning and many regiments produced their own cards. Christmas 1914 was not a

Right: In their heyday of the 1880s Christmas cards were advertised in the national newspapers, as shown in this advertisement from the 'Illustrated London News' of 1st December 1883.

Below: A folded card from the First World War with a cord tassel and a verse by E. Hutchings on the front. Inside, there is a pre-printed verse. (88 mm x 126 mm)

When the battle-cry rang through the land.
With the first our dear one took his stand.
On his picture now we gaze with pride.
While we pray God bless his Christmastide.

E. HUTCHINGS.

Right: *A distinctive folded card from the 1920s in the Grafton Series issued by The Medici Society. It has a strong Art Deco influence, after a design by Frank Sherwin, who was a watercolour painter in the 1920s and 1930s. (133 mm x 117 mm)*

Below: *A subdued card published by the Regional Petroleum Office for Christmas 1946. Inside (right) is a voucher for 'The RIGHT Spirit Unlimited Units' and a verse condemning the black market in petrol. (114 mm x 140 mm)*

The Season's Greetings

typical year for the volume of mail because of the problems of war, but in the six days up to 22nd December two and a half million letters and cards were posted.

After the First World War the cards of the 1920s and 1930s had a distinctive style inspired by the Art Deco movement, using the still popular designs of landscapes and snow-bound stagecoaches.

By comparison, Second World War cards were generally dull and lacking in colour due to austerity measures. However, at the beginning of the war, Christmas cards were still considered to be newsworthy and *The Times* continued to review them in great detail.

At the close of our period in Christmas 1946, in the week of 13th to 18th December, 3,450,000 letters and cards were posted in London and 15,605,000 in the provinces. The volume of Christmas mail had increased from 3,338,000 in London and 13,792,000 in the provinces in the previous year.

From their beginnings in 1843 until the end of the Second World War, the giving of Christmas cards became a favourite custom of the seasonal festivities because they were bright and colourful and, as the verse was pre-printed, the writer could send his or her greetings with the minimum of effort. They were miniature works of art and reflected the tastes and style of each decade.

A Merry Christmas and a Happy New Year.

THE VICTORIAN HEYDAY

Above left: *An unmarked card from the 1860s with a paper 'lace' border. The card features a roundel of a mother with children and a calligraphic border with the leaves printed in gold. (69 mm x 106 mm)*

Above right: *This small Christmas card with a scalloped paper 'lace' border was issued by Goodall & Son in the 1860s. The design features a robin, and the reverse is plain as this is where the message would have been written. (60 mm x 94 mm)*

To the Victorians, Christmas cards were like a breath of fresh air. They were colourful symbols of festive goodwill which *The Times* noted were 'the happy means of ending strifes, cementing broken friendships and strengthening family and neighbourhood ties...' Christmas cards were universally admired, especially by Queen Victoria, who gave them her royal seal of approval. In 1895 *Home Chat* recorded that: 'Not only does she procure at great expense cards for all her royal relatives...but she buys not less than thousands to send to her neighbours at Windsor and Osborne.'

The Victorians were avid collectors of all manner of things, not least Christmas cards. The hobby was especially popular with children but was also enjoyed by adults, and cards were kept in albums, often dated and titled with the sender's name.

Today's collector of Christmas cards will come across a wide variety of cards, some of which can be identified by the publisher's trademark, and others that are unmarked. Early Christmas cards of the 1850s were produced on a relatively small scale by publishers such as Kronheim, Dickes, Joseph Mansell and Leighton Brothers, many of whom were Baxter licensees (see page 8) and had produced Valentines for several years.

Charles Goodall & Son, in the early 1860s, was the first company to become known for Christmas card production. Most cards are marked with the company's trademark of a heart with the name 'Goodall' within it. The company started producing elaborate Christmas stationery in 1859 and the development into Christmas card production was a natural progression. Early cards were edged with paper 'lace' borders made by machine and were visiting-card size. The firm continued

Above: *A Goodall card from the early 1870s with a paper 'lace' border. This features 'Dr Yule's Popular Lectures for the Young' and is 'No. 1 The Globes'. Note that the globe is a Christmas pudding. (75 mm x 107 mm)*

producing cards for thirty years and was renowned for its fine printing.

Another publisher of the 1860s was Benjamin Sulman of London. He also made small cards edged with 'lace', engraved, embossed and die-stamped, but it is more difficult to find surviving examples of these.

In 1867 Marcus Ward, a Belfast publisher, opened a London office at Oriel House, Farringdon Street. The company became associated with publishing finely designed Christmas cards and employed such prestigious artists as Walter Crane and Kate Greenaway. Marcus Ward & Co stopped production of Christmas cards in the late 1890s.

Thomas De La Rue & Co (already mentioned in connection with envelope making) was founded in the 1820s and was chiefly known for making embossed paper bonnets, printed playing cards and banknotes. From about 1874 it diversified into Christmas card production. Its cards are often numbered, and artists included W. S. Coleman, J. M. Dealy and Ernest Griset. The company stopped producing Christmas cards in 1883.

Although this book is concerned with the history of the British Christmas card, it is worth mentioning Louis Prang, the 'Father of the American Christmas Card'. Prang was famous for inventing a system of colour printing using zinc plates instead of lithographic stones, and for brilliantly coloured cards, including examples with black and red backgrounds. In 1880 his company was the first to introduce competitions for Christmas card designs, and this was quickly copied in Britain by Raphael Tuck & Sons and others.

Raphael Tuck & Sons was the most prolific Christmas card manufacturer and was active right up to the end of the Second World War and

This card was issued by De La Rue & Co as Series Number 124 and is part of a set of three called 'Children at Play'. The card is dated 1878 on the reverse. (133 mm x 101 mm)

A trade card issued by Raphael Tuck in the 1870s which illustrates their wide range of services. (136 mm x 90 mm)

beyond. The company started producing cards in about 1871 and soon gained a reputation for raising the standard of designs by staging prestigious competitions. The 1880 competition attracted 925 entries. Tuck received a Royal Warrant in 1893 as publisher to Queen Victoria and continued to publish Christmas cards for the royal family after her death. Hundreds of series of cards were made, including the Artistic Series and the Royal Academic Series, which were of an extremely high quality.

Two well-known Christmas card publishers originated in Germany and started producing cards in the 1870s after emigrating to Britain. Siegmund Hildesheimer, who specialised in silvered, frosted and embossed cards, had offices in Manchester, London and New York. The other company, Hildesheimer & Faulkner, which was a partnership between Albert Hildesheimer and C. W. Faulkner, produced fine cards mixing silver with colours. The partnership was dissolved in 1893 but C. W. Faulkner continued to produce Christmas cards.

There are many well-known artists of Christmas cards, the majority of whom are also known for their book illustrations. Kate Greenaway designed Christmas cards and Valentines for a number of publishers including Kronheim, Marcus Ward and Goodall. Her distinctive designs of children in Regency costumes are instantly recognisable. John Ruskin praised her work in a lecture he gave in 1883 called 'Fairyland' and, after receiving a card from her, wrote: 'Luck go with you, pretty lass...To my mind it [the card] is a greater thing than Raphael's St Cecilia.'

Walter Crane was an illustrator of children's books and his style was influenced by the Pre-Raphaelites and Japanese prints. He was prominent in the Arts and Crafts Movement alongside William Morris and he designed cards for Marcus Ward.

William Stephen Coleman was another illustrator of books, mainly on natural history. His sister Rebecca was also involved in designing Christmas cards. Coleman's designs of scantily clad children prompted

WISHING YOU A MERRY CHRISTMAS!

Above: *A Raphael Tuck card from the 'Artistic Serie Number 167 issued in the 1880s. The card features view of the Houses of Parliament and a verse on the ba by Eliza Cook. (124 mm x 90 mm)*

Left: *A prize design issued by Raphael Tuck & Sons the early 1880s with a verse on the back by the Reverer Frederick Langbridge. (96 mm x 140 mm)*

Below: *This card in the shape of the crescent moon is or of a pair issued by S. Hildesheimer & Co in the 1880s. features a church scene designed by A. F. Lydon, wl specialised in designing 'shaped' cards including cross and circles. (130 mm x 56 mm)*

WITH ALL MY HEART I WISH YOU A HAPPY CHRISTMAS.

With the Season's Greetings

Above: *A card issued by S. Hildesheimer & Co featuring a gold border and a traditional Christmas scene of holly. This design is Number 231 and came third in a competition of the 1880s. (74 mm x 94 mm)*

Top left: *A humorous card issued by Hildesheimer &*
Faulkner in the 1880s (Number 968), designed in Eng-
land but printed in Germany. (99 mm x 138 mm)

Top right: *This card was issued by Robert Canton in*
1878 as part of a set that also featured a parrot, a cat,
mice and dogs. On the reverse is a cryptic message:
'Goodbye! I leave on Sunday next – fare thee well!!!
Ato [sic]. Acton 23-12-78' (80 mm x 116 mm)

Middle: *A card by Kate Greenaway issued by Marcus*
Ward & Co c.1880. The design features six girls hold-
ing a garland of roses and it was also used with a
different verse as a Valentine. (158 mm x 80 mm)

Left: *This card, designed by W. S. Coleman for De La*
Rue & Co, is from Series Number 307 and features a
girl with a lute. It is one of a set of three – the other two
designs are of a girl asleep on a cushion and a naked
child asleep on a sofa. (118 mm x 118 mm)

A highly decorative, unmarked card featuring a stunning design of calligraphy and ivy. It is dated 1874 on the reverse. (121 mm x 80 mm)

Right: An unmarked card with a paper 'lace' border featuring a mill scene and a robin. The card is dated on the reverse Christmas 1871. (69 mm x 112 mm)

Below: A card by Robert Canton, issued c.1877, with a black background and a boy appearing through a peephole. (70 mm x 108 mm)

this comment from *Punch* in 1878: '*Punch* must protest...against nudities at Christmas – it is too cold for them, if there were no other reason.'

Designs of Victorian Christmas cards were wonderfully varied. As we have seen, sending greetings at New Year was common before Christmas cards became popular, and many cards have distinctly pagan themes as a throwback to

An unmarked card from c.1880 which features two colourful robins. (116 mm x 73 mm)

WISHING YOU ALL THE PLEASURES OF THE SEASON.

Left and below: *A stunning, unmarked card with a gold, scalloped edge featuring a design of purple flowers. The card opens to reveal a colourful picture of a girl with a robin. (124 mm x 85 mm)*

that older tradition. Many designs, such as countryside scenes and studies of flowers, do not seem seasonal but they look forward to the coming spring and summer and are also common themes of the Valentine. In addition, the language of flowers was an important part of Victorian court-ship. For example, a Christmas card bearing a picture of a red chrysanthemum discreetly proclaimed 'I love you'.

Early cards reflected the tastes of the upper and upper middle classes, and scenes of hunting, fishing and shooting were hugely popular. Many cards were an early form of nostalgia, harking back to medieval and seventeenth-century England. The robin first appeared on a Christmas card in the 1850s and Father Christmas from the 1870s. Later, designs ranged from negroes and

Above: *A small, unmarked card from the 1890s featuring a scene of children at the seaside. The boys are wearing traditional sailor suits. (101 mm x 67 mm)*

Below left: *An unmarked card from the 1880s, designed by A. P., which pokes fun at the seriousness of the Aesthetic Movement. The greeting reads: 'Let me utter my quite too utter best wishes'. (75 mm x 121 mm)*

Below right: *An unmarked novelty card from the 1880s featuring an embossed cat mask. (83 mm x 111 mm)*

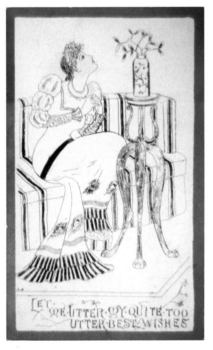

A shaped card issued by Robert Canton in the 1880s which shows a very popular motif of the time: blue and white china in the form of a teapot. (95 mm x 95 mm)

A three-dimensional Christmas card from c.1890 featuring a Nativity scene and a blue optical strip that, when held to the light, throws 'moonlight' on the back of the stable. (156 mm x 163 mm)

A shaped card issued by Raphael Tuck & Sons featuring a seascape by A. Wilde Parsons. (106 mm x 100 mm)

A humorous, unmarked card from the 1880s featuring three monkeys teasing a dog. (129 mm x 81 mm)

idealised Japanese scenes through to comic animals and cards poking fun at the Aesthetic Movement. Towards the end of the century, designs reflected the influences of Art Nouveau and the decadence of *fin de siècle*.

Victorian ingenuity was almost limitless. Cards were produced in every conceivable shape and size, from crescents and postboxes to the enormous 18 inch (45.7 cm) wide cards which in 1895 caused problems

Left: *This small, unmarked card has a gold background and shows that roller-skating was popular even in Victorian times. (70 mm x 95 mm)*

Below: *An unmarked, religious card from the 1890s featuring verses from Isaiah and Matthew. (124 mm x 90 mm)*

A card from 1885 issued by the German publisher Bernhard Ollendorff with a traditional snowy scene and a verse on the back by Roger Quiddam. (117 mm x 78 mm)

A folded, unmarked Christmas card with a decorative edge and a pre-printed space for both the sender's and the recipient's names inside. (73 mm x 128 mm)

for the Post Office. Tableaux, which opened to make a three-dimensional scene, and mechanical/tab cards were perennial favourites although they were more expensive than standard cards. Imitation cheques, 'purse' cards, silk-fringed cards and cards with 'squeakers' to make bird sounds were all popular in their time.

Many Victorian Christmas cards were printed in Germany because printing there was of such a high standard. In the 1890s adverse economic conditions and the vast number of German imports made German cards an enemy to British commerce, so that German publishers fell out of favour.

In the late Victorian period both Marcus Ward & Co and De La Rue & Co stopped producing Christmas cards because of concerns that artistic standards had dropped with the increase in mass production. Even so, Christmas cards never waned in popularity and entered the twentieth century as a favourite festive custom.

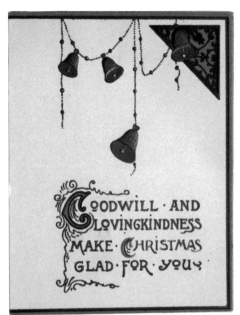

A small, folded card issued by Raphael Tuck & Sons in the 1890s for their Artistic series and printed in embossed red and gold with a verse inside by Ellis Walton. (73 mm x 94 mm)

Right: *A small, folded card with a scalloped edge and featuring a girl in blue. It was issued by Davidson Bros, designed in England but printed in Germany in the 1890s. (77 mm x 108 mm)*

Below: *A stunning unmarked card from 1880 with a tab mechanism that, when pulled, adds wings to the butterfly. Such cards are fragile and, although the butterfly is shown with a wing, the mechanism has broken and the other wing is missing. (120 mm x 80 mm)*

THE EDWARDIAN ERA AND THE FIRST WORLD WAR

The death of Queen Victoria in January 1901 brought Britain to the threshold of a new era. There was a real feeling that times were changing. Gone were the stuffy, straightlaced attitudes of the Victorians, and in came a freer, more fun-loving society. Very few of the Victorian publishers were still in business. Raphael Tuck & Sons established itself as the leading publisher of Christmas cards after Marcus Ward & Co and De La Rue & Co stopped production in the late nineteenth century.

As in Victorian times, Christmas cards remained an important feature of the Edwardian Christmas and *The Times* continued to review cards from publishers that were considered noteworthy.

New publishers included C. W. Faulkner & Co, Valentine & Sons, Hills & Co and Dennis & Sons. Many of these companies were publishers of postcards and were quick to produce Christmas versions for an eager Edwardian public. Christmas postcards were cheap and did not

A small card issued by Raphael Tuck & Sons featuring mistletoe and stars. The leaves, flowers and mistletoe berries are embroidered. (110 mm x 70 mm)

A card issued by M & Co (possibly Misch & Co) with a gold background and a section for a photograph to be inserted. This photograph was taken by Jewells of Wilton Chambers, Market Street, Manchester. (112 mm x 75 mm)

A small, folded card issued by Raphael Tuck & Sons featuring two embossed Japanese figures, reflecting the interest in all things Japanese. (73 mm x 93 mm)

Below: A humorous card (left) issued by Raphael Tuck & Sons of a baby's bottle that opens out to reveal a screaming baby (right). (95 mm x 148 mm when opened out)

26

Left: A Christmas postcard issued by C. W. Faulkner & Co (Series Number 886B) and postmarked 23rd December 1910. The card was designed in England but printed in Germany. (90 mm x 140 mm)

This charming Christmas card was issued in the 1880s by Raphael Tuck & Sons as No. 212 in the Artistic Series. On the back is a verse by H. M. Burnside. (90 mm x 132 mm)

require an envelope, and, as there was space for only a short message, even the less literate could send them. Despite their low cost, they were colourful, attractive and well printed. Huge numbers of sets were produced, especially by Raphael Tuck and C. W. Faulkner.

For the majority of publishers, Christmas cards were just a small part of their annual output. Alexander Baird & Son was an 'artistic stationery' manufacturer based in Glasgow, famous for its Golden Series of Christmas cards. The Medici Society, which was first registered in the *London Post Office Directory* in 1910, specialised in publishing art for the wider public. Throughout this period, Christmas card publishers were proud to state that their cards were designed and published in England rather than in Germany.

Top left: *An early postcard with an undivided back featuring a Christmas tree. The message is written on the front and the card is postmarked August 1904! (87 mm x 136 mm)*

Top right: *Poinsettia has long been a popular symbol of Christmas, as shown on this early Edwardian postcard printed in Saxony. (87 mm x 136 mm)*

Above: *A Raphael Tuck postcard in the 'Christmas Postcard Series', Number 8240, depicting a typical Edwardian nursery scene, showing two children with a rocking horse, abacus and other toys. (138 mm x 87 mm)*

Right: *A postcard featuring the perennial favourite, a robin, in the Raphael Tuck 'Oilette' Series, Number 8465. (138 mm x 88 mm)*

Christmas card designs reflected the decadence of the Edwardian period and many were excessively decorative. They were also influenced by Art Nouveau, the decorative style that was in vogue between about 1890 and 1910. Art Nouveau designs were in turn inspired by the simplicity and 'back to nature' style of the Arts and Crafts Movement and featured curving lines known as 'whiplash' in sinuous, stylised flowers and foliage.

Christmas cards were now folded and produced in vast quantities for the mass market. The cards were tied with ribbon or cord and were not as bright or as colourful as Victorian cards. In 1903 *The Times* reported that Raphael Tuck & Sons had produced 1600 entirely new

A Christmas postcard by Raphael Tuck & Sons which is Number 8411 in the Christmas Series. The design features a girl standing under the mistletoe with two boys wearing seventeenth-century costumes overlaid with gold. (139 mm x 88 mm)

Below left: An unmarked, folded card featuring a windmill scene and secured with a ribbon. (94 mm x 115 mm)

Below right: A small, folded card secured with a cord, in the Golden Series issued by Alexander Baird & Son. (76 mm x 98 mm)

A folded card issued by Raphael Tuck & Sons depicting John Wesley's armchair. The card is secured with a ribbon, and inside is a verse by Wesley. (140 mm x 88 mm)

Left: *A small, unmarked, folded card featuring an embossed dog and drum, dated 1909 on the back; designed in England but printed in Prussia. (69 mm x 89 mm)*

Below left: *This late Edwardian card has a hand-painted celluloid cover and would have been secured with a cord or ribbon. (112 mm x 108 mm)*

sets: one thousand in colour, four hundred in black and white and monochrome, and 'the remainder are painted flowers formed of satin and velvet raised over a surface of transparent celluloid'. This is an indication of the new types of materials that were used for manufacturing cards. Throughout the period until the First World War, designs featured relatively new inventions such as the aeroplane and the motor car, both symbols of the new-found Edwardian freedom and the growing influence of technology on society.

For a few months after the start of the First World War the government banned the sending of greetings cards for security reasons and as part of an economy drive for the war effort. *The Times* was concerned that 'it would be a great pity if as a result of the war the time honoured custom of exchanging greetings should be allowed to lapse'. However, it was soon realised that Christmas cards could boost morale and the royal family set the standard by continuing to send cards

Left and above: *A card issued by the 17th Division sent back from the front during the First World War. The inside of the card shows a humorous view of the war. (120 mm x 175 mm)*

throughout the war. In 1917 *The Times* reported that the sending of Christmas cards 'persists as a token of good fellowship'. Even so, economising was considered a great virtue and for many people Christmas cards were a luxury that could be done without. Certainly there was a marked decline in the number of Christmas cards sent during the war, offset by an increase in the number of parcels sent to the front.

There was a distinct change of mood in Christmas card design at the outbreak of the First World War. Cards featured less of the trappings of Edwardian decadence and showed a tendency towards greater simplicity. The main theme of First World War cards was patriotism. Many cards were secured with a red, white and blue ribbon or cord. There

The inside of a card issued by the 46th Division. It was printed in Manchester. (168 mm x 102 mm)

ARE WE
DOWN HEARTED? 'NO!'

Left: *A First World War card secured with a red, white and blue cord and featuring a patriotic bulldog design. (140 mm x 89 mm)*

Below left: *A simple First World War card secured with a red ribbon. (80 mm x 114 mm)*

Below right: *A First World War card sent to the front, secured with a red, white and blue cord. The verse inside reads: 'A Card I send for "Auld Lang Syne", To Cheer You in the fighting line.' (74 mm x 120 mm)*

To GREET You

LUCK BE WITH YOU

FONDEST GREETINGS FROM AFAR

were two different kinds of card: those sent to the front and those sent from the front. Most regiments issued their own cards to send back home, including silk embroidered postcards.

In 1916 it was announced that a Christmas card would be issued by the National War Savings Committee that would have space to affix one or more sixpenny stamps. This card combined sending festive greetings with aiding the war effort.

Throughout the war, *The Times* continued to review Christmas cards Publishers included Raphael Tuck & Sons, which remained the leading publisher, Valentine & Sons, Dennis & Sons, C. W. Faulkner & Co, Hills & Co, The Medici Society and A. R. Mowbray & Co.

A huge number of cards were pulped for the war effort so relatively few examples of cards from this period have survived.

A small, cream card from the 1930s featuring a woodcut design issued by the Gordon Fraser Gallery of Cambridge. (114 mm x 88 mm)

GREETINGS

THE INTER-WAR YEARS AND THE SECOND WORLD WAR

A card dated 1924 secured with a cord and with the words 'National Series' inside. (86 mm x 136 mm)

MAY CHRISTMAS JOYS
BE THICK AS
SNOWFLAKES

Between the two world wars there was another significant change in the style of Christmas cards. Designs were influenced greatly by Art Deco, the bold decorative style that was popular throughout the 1920s and 1930s. The distinctive features were clean lines and sharp edges in brightly coloured geometric patterns. Another style of card design revived the art of wood engraving and this was favoured by two new publishers, the Gordon Fraser Gallery and the Ward Gallery.

There was a new vogue for the reproduction of famous paintings on Christmas cards, and this method of bringing art to the people was led by The Medici Society. For Christmas 1918, the company issued a card that featured an autolithograph of 'The Oxen' by A. S. Hartrick accompanied by the complete text of Thomas Hardy's poem of that title, revised by the author.

In 1923 the British Museum added to the artistic nature of designs by issuing fifteen Christmas cards printed with reproductions of miniatures from medieval French and Flemish manuscripts depicting the Nativity and the Epiphany.

The 'typical' Christmas card, featuring a traditional snowy scene, had virtually disappeared. The cards that were being produced were of a high artistic standard despite the challenge of meeting the demands of the mass market. In 1926 *The Times* praised the beauty of design and the reproduction of fine pictures and argued that the Christmas card 'might well have gone the way of the Valentine after the war

An ornate card more reminiscent of a wedding card than a Christmas card. It is pre-printed with the sender's name and address for Christmas 1925. (82 mm x 96 mm)

if a change in the taste of the public had not been anticipated and encouraged'.

Private greetings cards pre-printed with the sender's name were the exception rather than the rule as the public increasingly saw Christmas cards as a personal way of sending good wishes and marking the festive season. There was a growing tendency to supplement Christmas cards with artistic calendars.

Humorous cards continued to be popular such as those published by Valentine & Sons featuring Mabel Lucie Attwell's designs of round-faced babies. There was still a demand for novelty cards such as the 1929 gramophone record card issued by Raphael Tuck.

W. Heffer & Sons of Cambridge issued many series of artistic cards. In 1930 they included the Burnham Abbey Series, which was 'modern, mystical and catholic', and the Cantabrigia Series of coloured pictures by Estella Canziani and ancient views of Cambridge.

A new publisher of the early 1930s was the Ward Gallery, which specialised in reproducing wood engravings and issued very attractive and cheap cards for no more than one shilling. Designs included winter landscapes, linocuts and snow scenes. Ward Gallery cards were economically printed, often in black or a single colour or in hand-separated colours with the use of tints.

An unmarked card from the 1920s secured with a tasse cord, featuring a deer scene. The card is pre-printed with the sender's initial on the front in ivy leaves. (118 mm x 97 mm

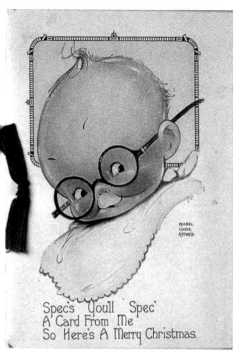

An unmarked card from the 1920s secured with a ribbon and featuring a design by Mabel Lucie Attwell. (98 mm x 140 mm)

Above and left: *A stunning triptych card in the Cantabrigia Series printed by W. Heffer & Sons of Cambridge. This features a design of Good King Wenceslas by HAZ. (Opened-out size: 217 mm x 180 mm)*

In the 1930s Raphael Tuck & Sons continued to be a leading publisher of cards and issued the 'pot-pourri lamp series', embroidered cameos, parchment etchings and bas-relief panelled greetings cards.

There were also charity Christmas cards, with the Royal Society for the Protection of Birds and the Norfolk Naturalist Trust both receiving mentions in *The Times*. In 1931 seventeen thousand RSPB cards were sold. Archibald Thorburn painted a series of cards for the RSPB, the last of which was of a goldcrest in 1935.

Publishers of this period also included Holly Bush Publications, Valentine & Sons, C. W Faulkner & Co, A. R. Mowbray & Co, A. M. Davis & Co, W. N. Sharpe Ltd and Raphael Tuck & Sons.

During this time, artists' names were not always mentioned on the cards but illustrators could work for a number of different publishers to keep up with demand. Rowland Hilder, who specialised in painting the English landscape,

Above: A striking card with an Art Deco design printed by the Ward Gallery in three colours. (93 mm x 127 mm)

Below left: A subdued card from the 1930s printed by A. M. Davis & Co. It proudly states that it is of 'British Manufacture'. (78 mm x 108 mm)

Below right: A 1920s card from Raphael Tuck & Sons secured with a ribbon and featuring an eastern roundel and parchment-style cover. (98 mm x 114 mm)

was contracted by both The Medici Society and the Ward Gallery to produce a number of Christmas card designs each year.

At the outbreak of the Second World War, Raphael Tuck & Sons was the only Christmas card publisher remaining from the Victorian heyday. In 1937 *The Times* commented that the firm provided 'something for every age, pocket and taste'. Other publishers were Valentine & Sons, J. Arthur Dixon, Holly Bush Publications, the Ward Gallery, The Medici Society and W. Heffer & Sons.

The sending of Christmas cards during the war took on a similar pattern to that of the First World War. There was again a marked decline in the number of cards sent, due to economising for the war effort, and an increase in the number of parcels.

A new form of Christmas greeting was the airgraph, which troops could use to send messages home. The service started in 1941 and the sender wrote his or her message in

Above: A 1920s card from Sharpe's Classic Series secured with a cord. (80 mm x 125 mm)

Below left: A small card from the 1920s in the 'National Series' featuring robins and holly. (77 mm x 110 mm)

Below right: An unmarked card from the 1930s with a strong Art Deco influence. It is secured with a cord. (123 mm x 102 mm)

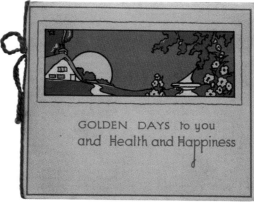

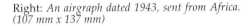

SEASON'S GREETINGS

Above: *A National Savings greetings card featuring four ladies in different historical costumes representing the seasons. Inside, the card reads: 'This card brings you the Season's greetings and a Savings gift towards the happier days that are coming.' (114 mm x 96 mm)*

Right: *An airgraph dated 1943, sent from Africa. (107 mm x 137 mm)*

the blank area of an illustrated sheet, handing it in at any post office. A photographic negative was taken of the message and despatched by airmail. At the destination a photographic print was made and delivered to the addressee.

During the Second World War and immediately afterwards the National Savings Movement issued thirty-five different designs of cards that combined 'utility with beauty'. They included traditional designs of flowers and stagecoaches, reproductions of paintings such as 'Stable Interior' by George Morland and 'The Boyhood of Raleigh' by Sir John Everett Millais, and a coloured reproduction of the symbol of the National Savings Movement's committee, a Fiery Cross. The cards were free of charge to purchasers of savings stamps and they contained thirty spaces to carry savings stamps worth either two shillings and sixpence or sixpence.

Throughout the hundred years since the first Christmas card, designs reflected the changes in the taste of the public and the artistic movements of the day, such as Arts and Crafts, Art Nouveau and Art Deco. In the beginning publishers had been concerned to raise the standard of artistic merit of the cards, and at the end of the period, despite the challenges presented by mass production, it was still possible to buy individual high-quality cards. The tradition of sending Christmas cards is now well established and, except for during the two world wars, has not waned in popularity.

FURTHER READING

Blair, Arthur. *Christmas Cards for the Collector*. Batsford, 1986.

Buday, George. *The History of the Christmas Card*. Spring Books, 1954. (No longer in print but the definitive work on the subject.)

Hillier, Bevis. *Greetings from Christmas Past*. Herbert, 1982.

Seddon, Laura. *A Gallery of Greetings: a Guide to the Seddon Collection of Greetings Cards in Manchester Polytechnic Library*. Manchester Polytechnic Library, 1992. (Useful for identifying cards when starting a collection. Manchester Polytechnic is now Manchester Metropolitan University.)

Staff, Frank. *The Picture Postcard and Its Origins*. Lutterworth Press, 1979.

Above left: *An unusual unmarked card from the early 1880s depicting serpents and featuring a religious verse by Milton. (120 mm x 95 mm)*

Above right: *An embossed folded card from the Edwardian period issued by Raphael Tuck & Sons. Inside, there is a short verse by Sir Walter Scott and a pre-printed 'from'. (95 mm x 150 mm)*

Places to Visit

Bodleian Library, Broad Street, Oxford OX1 3BG. The John Johnson Collection: telephone 01865 277047 (e-mail: jjcoll@bodley.ox.ac.uk) Admissions: telephone 01865 277180 (e-mail: admissions@bodley.ox.ac.uk) (Visitors can consult material from the John Johnson Collection by applying for a Bodleian reader's ticket and making an appointment with the supervisor of the collection.)

British Museum, Great Russell Street, London WC1B 3DG. Telephone: 020 7636 1555. (Visitors can view Queen Mary's Christmas Cards in the Study Room of the Prints and Drawings Department by appointment only.)

Manchester Metropolitan University Library, All Saints Building, All Saints, Manchester M15 6BH. Telephone: 0161 247 2000. (The Laura Seddon Collection in the library may be viewed by appointment only.)

Victoria and Albert Museum, Cromwell Road, South Kensington, London SW7 2RL. Telephone: 020 7938 8500. (No appointment is necessary to view the Christmas card collection in the Prints, Drawings and Paintings Department.)

City libraries, archive departments and small museums often have collections of Christmas cards in the form of albums that have been donated over the years by members of the public.

The Ephemera Society

The Society is a non-profit-making body concerned with the preservation, study and educational uses of printed and handwritten ephemera. It organises a number of Ephemera Fairs throughout the year in London, at which items can be bought and sold, and series of lectures and meetings. Members receive the Society's handbook, which lists names and addresses of other members with their collecting/curatorial interest, and a quarterly journal which carries news, articles and 'sales' and 'wants' announcements. Further information can be obtained from: The Ephemera Society, 8 Galveston Road, London SW15 2SA. Telephone/fax: 020 8874 3363.

This unmarked card dating from the 1880s combines the two Victorian sports of shooting and fishing. On the bottom of the card is a quote from Shakespeare: 'Prosper our sport'. (140 mm x 95 mm)